The Countries

The Philippines

Bob Italia

ABDO Publishing Company

visit us at
www.abdopub.com

Published by ABDO Publishing Company, 4940 Viking Drive, Edina, Minnesota 55435.
Copyright © 2003 by Abdo Consulting Group, Inc. International copyrights reserved in
all countries. No part of this book may be reproduced in any form without written
permission from the publisher.

Printed in the United States.

Photo Credits: Corbis
Contributing Editors: Tamara L. Britton, Kristin Van Cleaf, Stephanie Hedlund
Art Direction & Maps: Neil Klinepier

Library of Congress Cataloging-in-Publication Data

Italia, Bob, 1955-
    The Philippines / Bob Italia.
      p. cm. -- (Countries)
    Includes index.
    Summary: Provides an overview of the history, geography, people, economy,
government, and other aspects of life in the Philippines.
    ISBN 1-57765-842-6
    1. Philippines--Juvenile literature. [1. Philippines.] I. Title. II. Series.

DS655 .I83 2002
959.9--dc21

                                         2002018767

Contents

Halo!

Hello from the Philippines! The **Republic** of the Philippines is a country in the southwest Pacific Ocean. It is made up of more than 7,000 islands. Manila is the nation's largest city.

The Philippine government is a republic. It is ruled by the **constitution** of 1987. Filipinos elect their president. The Senate and the House of Representatives make the nation's laws.

The people of the Philippines speak English and Filipino. Almost all are Catholic, but some are Protestant or Muslim.

People have lived in the Philippines for more than 30,000 years. In the 1500s, Spain conquered the Philippines. Later, the United States governed the country.

The Philippines became an independent nation on July 4, 1946. Today, the government and the people are working together to make the Philippines a great place to work and live.

Halo *from the Philippines!*

Fast Facts

OFFICIAL NAME: Republic of the Philippines (Republika ng Philipinas)
CAPITAL: Manila

LAND
- Area: 115,830 square miles (300,000 sq km)
- Highest Peak: Mount Apo 9,692 feet (2,954 m)
- Lowest Point: Philippine Sea (sea level)
- Major River: Cagayan River

PEOPLE
- Population: 82,841,518 (July 2001 est.)
- Major Cities: Manila, Caloocan, Davao
- Languages: Filipino, English
- Religions: Catholicism, Protestantism, Islam

GOVERNMENT
- Form: Republic
- Head of Government: President
- Legislature: House of Representatives and Senate
- Flag: Two horizontal bands, blue and red, with a triangle on the mast side. Inside the triangle is a yellow sun with eight rays. In the corners of the triangle are yellow, five-pointed stars.
- Independence: July 4, 1946

ECONOMY
- Agricultural Products: Rice, coconuts, sugarcane, bananas, pineapples; pork, eggs, beef, fish
- Mining Products: Timber, petroleum, nickel, cobalt, silver, gold, salt, copper
- Manufactured Products: Textiles, drugs, chemicals, wood products, processed foods, petroleum products
- Money: Philippine peso (1 peso = 100 centavos)

MANILA

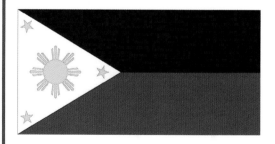

The Philippine's flag

Timeline

1521	Ferdinand Magellan claims the Philippines for Spain
late 1800s	Filipinos rebel against Spanish rule
1898	Emilio Aguinaldo starts rebel government; the U.S. wins the Spanish-American War, takes possession of the Philippines
1935	The Philippines becomes a commonwealth; Manuel Quezon is elected president
1942	Japanese invade during World War II
1946	The Philippines gains independence; Manuel Roxas elected president
late 1940s	People's Liberation Army attempts a government takeover
1954	PLA defeated
1965	Ferdinand Marcos elected president
1972	Marcos declares martial law
1983	Benigno Aquino killed
1986	Corazon Aquino becomes president
1987	Filipinos adopt new constitution
1989	Marcos dies
1992	Fidel Ramos elected president
1996	Peace agreement with Muslims signed
1998	Joseph Estrada elected president
2000	Gloria Macapagal-Arroyo becomes president

Philippine Past

Ferdinand Magellan

People have lived in the Philippines for nearly 30,000 years. Scientists believe people first **migrated** to the islands from other parts of Asia.

In 1521, explorer Ferdinand Magellan claimed the Philippines for Spain. The Spaniards named the islands after King Philip II. Spanish **missionaries** soon brought Christianity to the Filipinos.

In the late 1800s, the Filipinos **rebelled** against Spanish rule. In 1898, Emilio Aguinaldo (ah-gee-NAHL-doh) set up a rebel government. But that same year, Spain lost the Spanish-American War. Spain signed the Treaty of Paris, which gave control of the Philippines to the United States.

Manuel Quezon

The U.S. governed the Philippines until 1935. That year, the Philippines became a **commonwealth**. The people elected Manuel Quezon (KAY-sawn) president. In 1942, during **World War II**, Japanese forces invaded the Philippines. Quezon fled to the U.S., where he died in 1945.

That same year, the U.S. regained control of the Philippines. On July 4, 1946, the U.S. granted the Philippines independence. Filipinos elected Manuel Roxas (RAW-haws) president.

But not all Filipinos were happy with the new government. During the late 1940s, a **communist** group called the

Manuel Roxas

Ferdinand Marcos

People's Liberation Army tried to take over the government. But the Philippine Army defeated the group in 1954.

In 1965, Filipinos elected Ferdinand Marcos (MAHR-cohs) president. Under his leadership, new schools and roads were built. Agricultural production increased, and the **economy** improved. He was re-elected in 1969.

But social unrest continued. In the late 1960s and early 1970s, the **communist** New People's Army attacked military bases. And Muslims in the south **rebelled**. They wanted independence for Muslim areas. Marcos declared **martial law** in 1972 to gain control of the country.

In 1973, Marcos announced that a new **constitution** made him both president and **prime minister** for an unlimited term. This new law upset many Filipinos who were unhappy with Marcos's leadership. He put people who were against him in jail. And he took their money and property.

In 1977, most Filipinos favored Senator Benigno Aquino (uh-KEE-noh) to win the presidential election. So Marcos put him in jail. In 1980, Aquino was allowed to go to the U.S. for health care.

In 1983, Aquino was killed when he returned to the Philippines. U.S. leaders said he had been shot by **communists**. Aquino's followers said that the Philippine government was behind the killing.

Meanwhile, the **economy** was declining. Filipinos wanted a new leader. So in February 1986, a presidential election was held. Aquino's widow Corazon was Marcos's chief opponent.

After the election, the National Assembly ruled that Marcos had won. But many Filipinos accused Marcos of

Corazon Aquino

cheating. Thousands of people protested the election. Marcos fled the country for the U.S.

Corazon Aquino took over as president. She promised a more **democratic** government. In February 1987, Filipinos approved a new **constitution**. In 1989, Marcos died in the U.S. In 1992, Fidel Ramos (RAH-mohs) became president.

Meanwhile, Muslim **rebel** groups continued to fight for independence. In 1996, the government and the largest rebel group signed a peace agreement. They agreed to organize a region of self-rule in the southern part of the country. Despite this agreement, fighting continued.

In 1998, Joseph Estrada (ay-STRAH-thuh) was elected president. The next year, the Marcos family agreed to pay $150 million to victims of human rights abuses during Marcos's administration.

In 2000, Filipinos accused Estrada of **corruption**. But he denied the charges and refused to resign. So the House of Representatives voted to **impeach** him. The Senate began the trial, but Estrada stepped down. He was replaced by vice president Gloria Macapagal-Arroyo (mah-cah-PAH-guhl uh-ROY-oh).

Joseph Estrada

Gloria Macapagal-Arroyo

Island Nation

The Philippines is located in the south Pacific Ocean. The nation is an **archipelago** of over 7,000 islands. The islands are the tops of volcanoes that rose from beneath the sea.

Lowlands are found along the islands' coasts. Some islands have wide, inland plains. On the larger islands, volcanoes rise in the interior.

Many of the volcanoes are active. In 1991, Mount Pinatubo erupted, killing hundreds of people. The Philippines highest mountain, Mount Apo (AH-poh), is on Mindanao Island. It rises 9,692 feet (2,954 m) above the Pacific Ocean.

The Philippine Islands have many bays and harbors. The country's largest lakes are Laguna de Bay and Lake Sultan Alonto. Most Philippine rivers flow only during the rainy season.

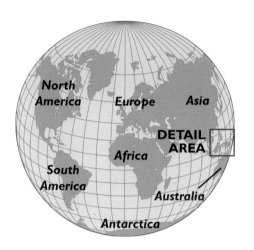

North America
Europe
Asia
Africa
South America
Australia
Antarctica
DETAIL AREA

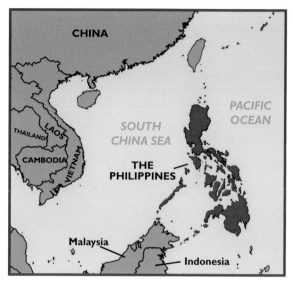

CHINA
PACIFIC OCEAN
LAOS
THAILAND
SOUTH CHINA SEA
CAMBODIA
VIETNAM
THE PHILIPPINES
Malaysia
Indonesia

LUZON
Mount Pinatubo
Caloocan
Laguna de Bay
MANILA
MINDANAO
Lake Sultan Alonto
Mount Apo
Davao
Philippine Trench

North
West — East
South

The Philippine Trench lies off the coast of the island of Mindanao. At 34,578 feet (10,539 m) deep, it is the second greatest depth known in any ocean.

The Philippine Islands have a hot, **humid** climate. The hottest months are from March to May. Temperatures cool during the rainy season. Damaging **typhoons** hit the Philippines each year.

A tropical rain forest on Panay Island

Rain

AVERAGE YEARLY RAINFALL

Inches		*Centimeters*
Under 20		*Under 50*
20 - 59		*50 - 150*
Over 59		*Over 150*

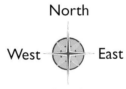

North

West — East

South

Summer

Winter

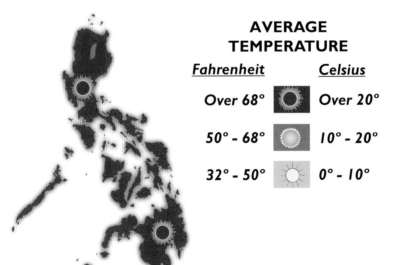

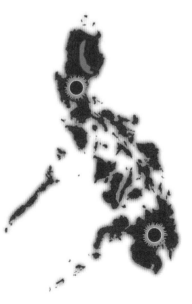

AVERAGE TEMPERATURE

Fahrenheit		*Celsius*
Over 68°		*Over 20°*
50° - 68°		*10° - 20°*
32° - 50°		*0° - 10°*

Wild Things

The Philippines's varied land and warm climate provide homes for many plants and animals. About half of the land is covered with forests. Banyan, pine, and palm trees grow in the forests. There are also tropical rain forests in the Philippines.

Thick groves of bamboo are common in the Philippines. About 9,000 kinds of flowering plants grow throughout the islands. They include 1,000 types of orchid.

Wild animals in the Philippines include crocodiles, monkeys, snakes, and many species of tropical birds. Tarsiers (TAHR-see-uhrz) are small mammals with owl-like eyes. Tarsiers live only in the Philippines and East Indies.

Carabaos (kar-uh-BAUHZ) are important **domestic** animals. Farmers use this type of water buffalo to pull plows, haul loads, and perform other tasks.

Tarsiers are only six inches (15 cm) long, but they can jump more than six feet (2 m)!

Filipinos

Almost all of the people in the Philippines are Filipino. The Negritos, whose **ancestors** settled in the islands about 30,000 years ago, live in small mountain villages. Chinese people make up the second largest group. Americans, Europeans, Indians, and Japanese also

An urban Filipino family

live on the islands, and have contributed to Philippine **culture**.

The Philippines has two official languages, Filipino and English. Filipinos speak about 70 native dialects of Filipino. Most Filipinos also speak English. English is widely used in business and government.

The Philippines has more Christians than any other Asian country. Most Filipinos are Catholic. The nation also has many Protestants and Muslims.

Most Filipinos have large families. Family members, including elder relatives and distant cousins, often have close relationships. Men hold most positions of

English	Filipino
Yes	Óo (OH)
No	Hindî (heend-E)
Thank you	Salámat (sahl-AH-maht)
Please	Pakí (pahk-EE)
Hello	Halo (hahlo)
Good-bye	Paalám (pahl-AH-m)

LANGUAGE

authority at home and in business. But many women work outside the home.

Western-style clothing is popular in the Philippines. But on holidays and other special occasions, some families wear traditional clothing. Men wear an embroidered shirt called a *barong tagalog* (BAH-rahng TAGA-log). Women wear a long dress called a *balintawak* (bahlin-TAH-wahk).

Filipino families live in both cities and rural areas. Most rural houses have wooden walls, thatch or metal roofs, and are grouped together. In the cities, government housing projects are common. So, too, are the slums, where poor families live in shacks. Wealthy families often live in large houses surrounded by protective walls.

Close family ties mean Filipino families eat together often. Many dishes are highly seasoned and spicy. A popular dish is *adobo,* made of chicken or pork cooked in vinegar and spices. Most Filipinos eat rice at every meal.

A Filipino family enjoys lunch together.

Children from 7 to 12 years old must attend school through the sixth grade. Public elementary school teachers instruct their students in the local dialect for the first two years. Then students begin to learn Filipino and English.

Adobo

Adobo is the Philippine national dish.

- 3 pounds pork
- 1 small onion, chopped
- 4 cloves garlic, minced
- 1 teaspoon peppercorns
- 1 or 2 bay leaves

- 1 cup vinegar (or enough to cover the meat)
- 4 tablespoons soy sauce
- 1 tablespoon salt

Cut the pork into 1 to 2 inch pieces. Combine all ingredients in a heavy saucepan. Bring to a boil, then reduce heat and simmer until the meat is tender and all the liquid has evaporated. When the liquid is all gone, continue cooking until the meat is browned, stirring occasionally. Serve hot with rice.

AN IMPORTANT NOTE TO THE CHEF: Always have an adult help with the preparation and cooking of food. Never use kitchen utensils or appliances without adult permission and supervision.

Instruction at most private schools, high schools, and universities is in English. University students must pass an English examination when applying for admission.

About one-third of college-age Filipinos attend college. The nation's largest university is Manila's University of the East.

Filipino children in school

Splendid Cities

Manila is the capital and largest city in the Philippines. About two million people live there. It is the country's busiest port, and the main **cultural**, social, business, and educational center.

Manila's major exports are electronic products, clothing and **textiles**, and processed foods. Other exports include minerals and timber products.

American, European, and Asian corporations have built large manufacturing businesses in Manila. These facilities produce electronics, drugs, and processed foods.

The city of Caloocan is located north of Manila. About one and a half million people live there. It is part of the district known as Metropolitan Manila.

Caloocan is one of Luzon Island's commercial, industrial, and educational centers. The city has factories, **textile** mills, small businesses, schools, and government offices.

Davao is on Mindanao island. More than one million people live there. It is Mindanao's commercial and trading center. Corn, abaca, pineapples, and timber are some of its main export products.

Manila's skyline at sunset

Making Money

Most Filipinos make their living in agriculture, forestry, mining, and fishing. Many also work in service industries, such as education, government, medicine, transportation, communication, and business. A few work in manufacturing.

Most of the Philippines's land is mountainous. So some farmers must raise crops on hillsides and mountain slopes. Filipino farmers produce almost all of the country's food. Rice and corn are the most important crops. Farmers also grow sweet potatoes, sugarcane, cassava, and fruits.

The Philippine government controls the nation's forestry industry. Almost all of the harvested lumber comes from the Luan tree. The Luan tree is a valuable tree from the rain forest. It is known as Philippine mahogany. Mangrove and pine trees also yield lumber.

A terraced rice field grows on the side of a mountain.

Mining is another important Philippine industry. Copper is the leading mineral. People mine gold in northern Luzon. The country also has deposits of chromite, coal, iron ore, limestone, manganese, nickel, silver, and zinc.

A Filipino fisherman with his nets

Since the Philippines is an island nation, many Filipinos earn a living by fishing. They catch anchovies, mackerel, sardines, tuna, and other fish in the waters around the islands. Crabs and shrimp are also harvested from the island waters.

Divers gather sponges and shellfish, including oysters and clams. Filipinos raise milkfish, shrimp, and tilapia in ponds.

The Philippines's main industrial products are cement, chemicals, cigars, and clothing. Other manufactured products include foods and beverages, refined metals and **petroleum**, sugar, **textiles**, and wood products.

A farmer planting rice

Getting Around

The Philippines has a good road system. But most Filipinos do not own automobiles. In most cities, people use buses, or cram into brightly-decorated vehicles called Jeepneys.

Much of the Philippines's railway system is located on Luzon Island. An elevated light-rail rapid transit system operates in the Manila area.

To move passengers and goods from island to island, ships and airplanes are used. The Philippines's major international airport is in Manila.

There are about 20 daily newspapers on the islands. Most of them are published in English. Other newspapers are printed in Filipino, Chinese, or other languages.

Most Filipinos own a television. They have several television stations to choose from.

The first Jeepneys were made from Jeeps that were abandoned in the Philippines at the end of World War II.

Philippine Government

The Philippines is a **republic**. All citizens who are at least 18 years old may vote in elections. The country is governed by the **constitution** of 1987. It divides power between executive, legislative, and judicial branches of government.

In the executive branch, the president is the head of government. The people elect the president. He or she is limited to one six-year term.

The legislative branch is made up of a two-house congress. The Senate has 24 members. Filipinos elect senators to six-year terms.

The House of Representatives has a maximum of 250 members. Voters elect 200 of them to three-year terms. The other 50 representatives are selected by the political parties. This assures representation of women, minorities, and other groups.

Locally, the Philippines is divided into 15 regions. Each is governed by a regional council. The regions are divided into 73 **provinces**. Every province has a governor, a vice governor, and two provincial board members. Filipinos elect these officials to four-year terms.

Philippine presidents live in Malacanany Palace in Manila.

Philippine Culture

The Philippines has rich **cultural** traditions. Many are kept alive in the country's museums. The Bureau of Science and the National Museum have collections of artifacts related to Philippine **folklore** and popular beliefs.

Art and literature are important ways that Philippine culture is passed on through generations. In the 1800s, Fabian de la Rosa (day lah ROH-zuh) was a popular Philippine artist. His favorite subject was the everyday life of Filipinos. Fernando Amorsolo (ah-mohr-SOH-loh) was one of de la Rosa's students. In the 1900s, he became famous for his portraits and rural landscapes.

Children on a slide

In the 1900s, José Rizal (hoh-SAY rih-ZAHL) wrote novels that criticized Spanish rule in the Philippines. Renato Constantino published essays that helped shape the national identity of the Philippines.

José Rizal

Filipinos have a rich **folklore** tradition. Some popular myths and legends address the creation of the world and the first man and woman on earth. Other tales tell of the Spanish conquest.

Organizations such as the Conservation Society and the **Cultural** Center of the Philippines help preserve Filipino folklore and history. Museums can be found in most **provinces**.

Glossary

ancestor - a person from whom one is directly descended.

archipelago - a group of islands.

commonwealth - a nation, state, or other political unit governed by the people for the common good.

communism - a social and economic system in which everything is owned by the government. A person who supports this system is a communist.

constitution - the laws that govern a country.

corrupt - to be influenced by other people to be dishonest.

culture - the customs, arts, and tools of a nation or people at a certain time.

democracy - a governmental system in which the people vote on how to run the country.

domestic - animals that are tame.

economy - the way a nation uses its money, goods, and natural resources.

folklore - tales, beliefs, customs, or other traditions of a people that are handed down from one generation to the next.

humid - having moisture or dampness in the air.

impeach - to have a trial to determine if a person should be removed from office.

martial law - law administered by government enforcement agencies, such as an army, when civilian enforcement agencies, such as police, can't maintain public order and safety.

migrate - to move from one place to settle in another.

missionary - a person who spreads a church's religion.

petroleum - a thick, yellowish-black oil. It is the source of gasoline.

prime minister - the highest-ranked member of some governments.

province - one of the main divisions of a country.

rebel - to disobey an authority or the government.

republic - a form of government in which power rests with voting citizens, and is carried out by elected officials such as a parliament.

textiles - of or having to do with the designing, manufacturing, or producing of woven fabric.

typhoon - a severe tropical hurricane in the western Pacific Ocean. Typhoons usually occur in late summer and early autumn.

World War II - 1939 to 1945, fought in Europe, Asia, and Africa. The United States, France, Great Britain, the Soviet Union, and their allies were on one side. Germany, Italy, Japan, and their allies were on the other side. The war began when Germany invaded Poland.

Web Sites

Would you like to learn more about the Philippines? Please visit **www.abdopub.com** to find up-to-date Web site links about the country's government and people. These links are routinely monitored and updated to provide the most current information available.

Index